My Pain Became Hers

Abigail Harrison

Further information and contact details can be found at the following websites:

www.anisianpublishing.com

ISBN: 978-1-7397962-9-7

ANISIAN | Publishing

Dedication

A book I'd like to dedicate to my daughter, whom I owe my life to.

Novaa-Jayde

We were never here nor there,
Never satisfied in each others love
At least you never were
I loved you,
I loved you enough for the both of us

Somewhere between the denial of
love
came the two lines you'd always
dreaded.
The lines I always dreamed of.

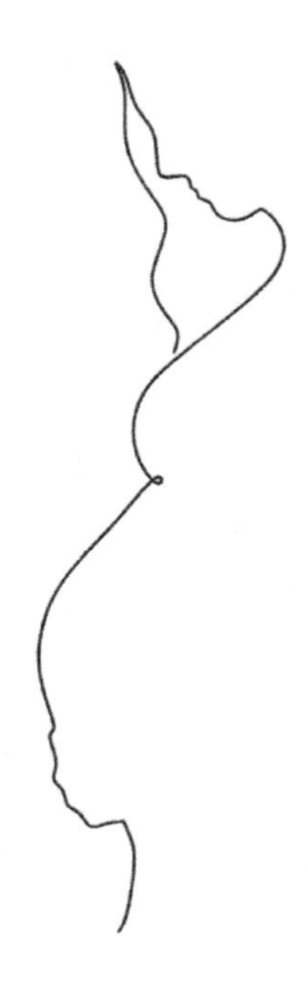

"Me or this"
my only options,
The double ended sword to my heart
Two people I loved more than life.
I had to choose one,
I chose HER

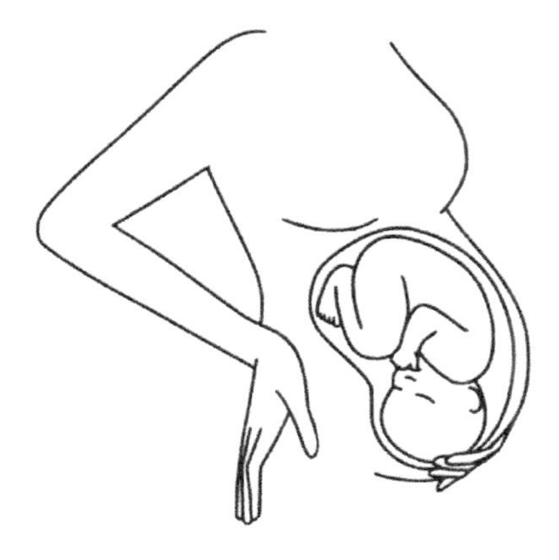

Two people lay down in love vs lust,
Only one person woke up and continued to
choose love over and over.
Maybe that's lust too...
Lusting for you to one day love me how I
have loved you for so long

As my belly began to grow,
My heart began to break
"It'll be okay"
Became a nightly prayer as I brushed away my own tears

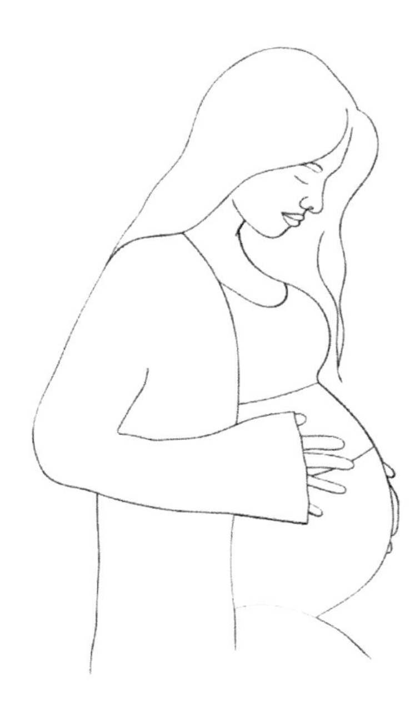

Nothing prepared me for the hardship you
skipped away from
A feeling of euphoria I never felt the way I
was supposed to
I couldn't say that though right ?
After all I chose this

My Pain Became Hers

As my belly began to grow
My heart began to freeze over
I knew if I felt too much she'd feel it too

The waiting rooms I longed for you to walk in and
hold my hand,
The sickness I longed for you to rub my back,
The bursts of pink smoke I looked for you in
longing for you to hug me in excitement,
The way I simply would cry in heartache longing
for your touch,
The birth, oh the birth the way I longed for you to
be there every step of the way,
The fact is I longed for you so much to love me
the way I loved you I forgot how much the life
inside me was feeling that way too

The endurance of such emotional pain,
Is a pain I hope you wouldn't want your daughter to feel ...
Again

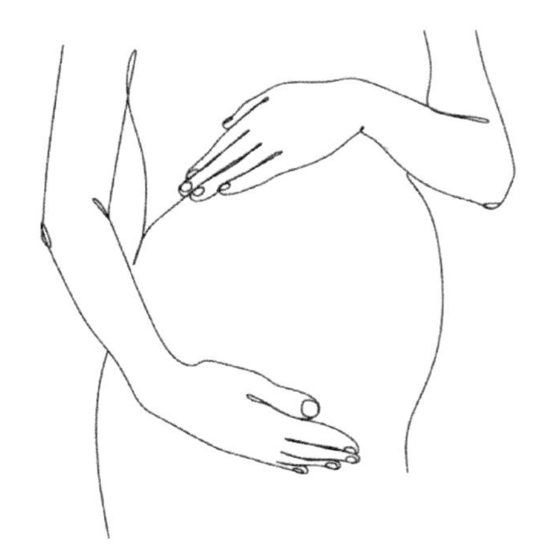

My heart aches for you,
Her heart aches for my pain

My pain was now hers

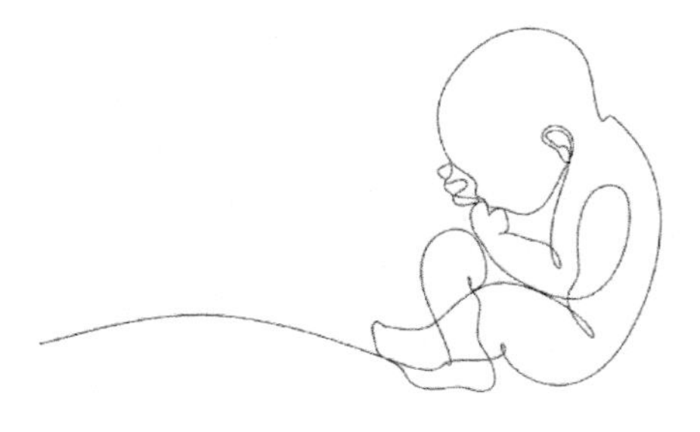

We flirt with the thin line between
love and hate,
Being sure not to cross it, not even for
a second
We both know how it goes

Nights I prayed for you,
For your forgiveness,
Your love,
Your happiness,
Your safety,
Nights I prayed for you while I wasn't a
second thought in your mind

I looked at her scans picking apart every
feature that reminds me of you.
Her cute button nose
"Doesn't she look just like ****"
I'd say over and over
A part of me hoped she would look like
you just to see you again
Guess that's my selfish thoughts tho
right ?

People say how brave and strong I must
be to do it alone.
A mask I learned to paint on so well,
If they could see the shattered pieces of
myself they'd have a different
perspective

9 months of love for most
9 months of guilt and upset for some

Sometimes when I lay in bed at night staring at the most precious gift I feel my pillow getting wet,
Tears I once cried out of anger and hurt are no more
Instead they're filled with overwhelming amounts of love for the 10 tiny fingers and toes that lay in front of me

My heart used to ache for you
The feeling of abandonment,
Worthlessness
Now my heart aches for you,
The loss you'll eventually feel of not feeling her
warm skin press into yours, seeing a smile from
ear to ear because you walked into the room.
My heart will always ache

I know now how selfish I was,
I didn't crave you to be her dad
I craved you for me,
To not abandon me like everyone before

The blood that ran through my veins,
Ran through hers.
The food I ate,
Fed her.
The music I listened to,
Soothed her.
Every step I took,
She came with me.
Every smile I smiled,
She felt the joy.
Every laugh I cried,
She felt the happiness.
Every tear I wept,
She felt the sorrow.
Every ounce of emotion that surged through me,
She felt with me.

To grieve the end of us was the worst
pain,
To leave you behind with a part of you
growing inside of me made me numb.
The numbness I felt for what never
would be,
Well it turned my heart to ice.

I loved you,
I thought I knew you,
But you can't hurt someone you love.

I guess I never really knew you,
Which means I never really loved you.

Just the idea of loving who I thought you were.

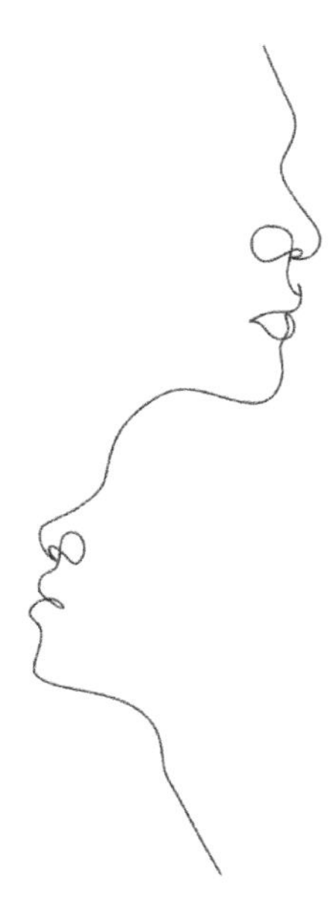

The fear angered you,
Angered you to the point of hatred.
Only not towards me,
No matter how much you tried it was never about me.
The loss of control,
Lack of understanding,
Raged through your body,
Only not towards me.
No matter how much you wanted to hate me,
It was never about me.

Why wasn't we Fucking enough for you?

I wouldn't say she's a burden,
Far from it.
I wouldn't say she's a mistake,
Far from it.
I wouldn't say she ruined things,
Far from it.
I wouldn't say she doesn't look like you,
She does.
I wouldn't say she doesn't remind me of you,
She does.
I wouldn't say she doesn't know about you,
She does.

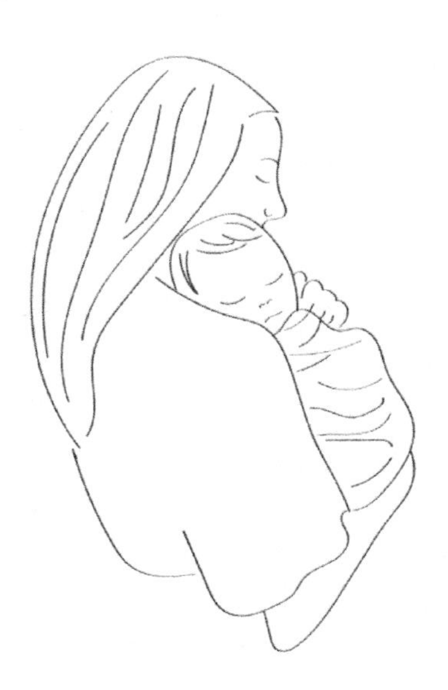

Hate you?
How could I hate you ?
Without you there would be no her and for that,
I love you

Many of times I cut my own hands
squeezing harder and harder to the
dagger between my chest.
Not trying to pull it out, oh no...
Trying to keep it in.
I knew for as long as I didn't pull it out
my heart wouldn't bleed.
For as long as I felt the pain I knew you
were real,
My feelings were real,
My memories were real,
For as long as I felt the pain I knew
everything was real.
How could I be so selfish ?

When two people so damaged by love meet each
other it was never going to end well.
Who was we trying to kid?
I fell in love with what could've been,
I romanticised a fantasy.
You fell in love with the pedestal I put you on,
You fell in love with the fact you'd always have
someone.
Even if it wasn't who you wanted.

Times I questioned myself
Maybe I'm too fat,
Maybe my hairs too short,
Maybe it's me,
Maybe it's the choice I made,
Maybe my eyes are too wide.
Times I questioned myself of why I was never
enough to be loved by you.

If you think your absence is loud,
It's not.
Your absence makes me know I can do it alone,
I'm a great mother.
That's not to say I don't talk about you,
I tell her everyday how much she looks like
you and how much I miss you.
The great thing about her is she already
knows,
For my pain was once hers.

Help me let you go.

Where do I find the time to think about you?
My days are busy.
My days are full of toys, laughter and tears.
My days are loud.
Where do I find the time to think about you ?
My nights are slow.
My nights are full of scrolling.
My nights are deafening with silence.
Night time is when I think about you the most

I guess a part of me,
The silliest part of me is still hoping.
Hoping for everything that could've been.

"I miss him"
No you miss the illusion you created

"She needs her dad"
No she needs love,
Stop chasing what you never had.

People said I deserved better,
I knew this may of been true,
I just wanted you to be better.

I just want to show you the love we never had.
We can be better.

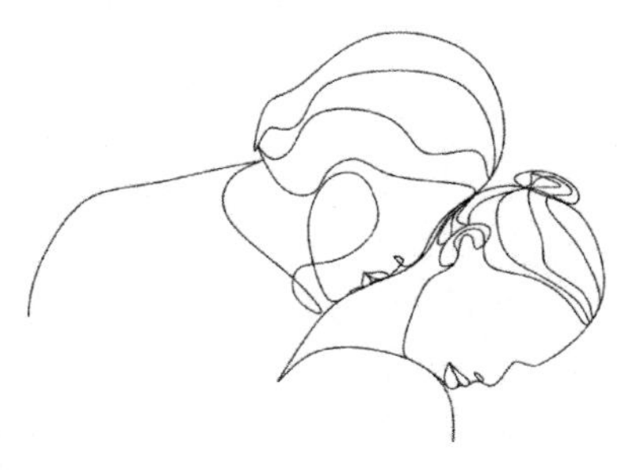

You moved on while I was carrying her,
With the girl who tried to befriend me.

When I say I hate him,
I don't mean I hate him,
What I mean is...

I hate how safe he made me feel in his presence,
I hate how much I missed it when it was no longer there,
I hate how the silence between us is louder than the words
we ever spoke to each other.

When I say I hate him,
I don't mean I hate him,
What I mean is...

I hate the opportunities I missed holding onto him,
I hate that he brought out the little girl inside of me
waiting for his call,
I hate that I don't need him but my heart only feels whole
when I'm with him.

When I say I hate him,
I don't mean I hate him,
What I mean is...

I hate that he's missing out on something so amazing,
I hate the fact he isn't around,
I hate that no matter how hard I try I still love him.

I hate him ...

After all the hurt I still see so much good in you.

The you I fell in love with is why I hold on.
I know this isn't you ...
Or maybe it always was

You call me crazy,
The truth is I was only ever crazy for you.

Teach me how ...
Teach me how I can forget you,
Teach me how I can let you go,
Teach me how I can wash away your touch,
Teach me how I can unlearn your habits,
Teach me how I can unlove you.

You seek validation in girls,
So much so you've never held your baby.

You think being a dad makes you weak ?
You're worried about what others think?
I know in my heart of hearts,
That's not it at all...
It wasn't in your plan,
You can't give a child what you didn't have,
Not because of weakness or Shame,
Simply because you don't know how.
How can you be the perfect role model ,
When yours was hidden in the shadows.

I forgive you,
She'll forgive you,
I'll always love you.

I don't hate the way you lack understanding,
I hate that you never try.

Don't wake up when it's too late,
What you have right in front of you might of
passed the sell by date.

I hold on to the idea of "maybe he will"

I know he won't

I gave you every ounce of me,
At no real cost to you,
A cost to me.
I gave you every ounce of me,
A gift to you,
A gift that cost me my heart.

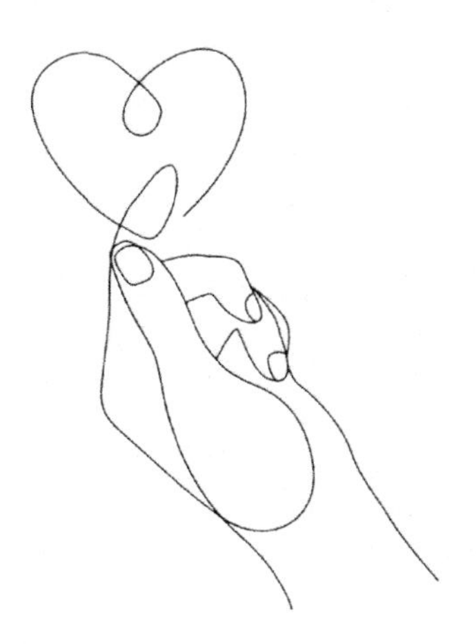

I had no idea falling in love with your eyes would
lead me to fall in love with myself

I wish you knew how much I love you,
I wish you knew how my heart drops
when I see your name,
I wish you knew how much it breaks me
every time you leave,
Oh how I wish you knew so much.
Even if you knew all of this,
I knew you wouldn't care.

My face smiles,
While my heart cries.
I have to be strong I can't show I'm
hurting,
The reality of that is she already knows.
She felt the sadness run through the
blood we once both shared,
She still knows now,
No matter how much I pretend I'm okay.
She knows my heart still cries for you.

I miss you ...

I wish I didn't

What was it about me that you couldn't commit to?
What is it about me that you can't let me go ?
You don't want me but won't let me leave.
So I stay in hopes I'll one day be enough,
The day that never seems to come...

I feed your ego and that's all I ever was to you,
Every inch of my body craved you,
For me and for her.
I feed your ego that's all I ever was to you.

I think it's crazy I still believe your lies,
"Maybe he's telling the truth",
I knew you never were,
For a moment it was nice to pretend everything was okay.
I think it's crazy we do a lot of talking but we never really say much,
We talk but nobody listens.
I think it's crazy that we never really spoke at all,
Our body's done the talking,
Since your hands don't graze over the surface of my skin anymore there's no conversation to be had anymore.
I think it's crazy.

How do you tell someone you can't just let them go ?

no matter how hard you try

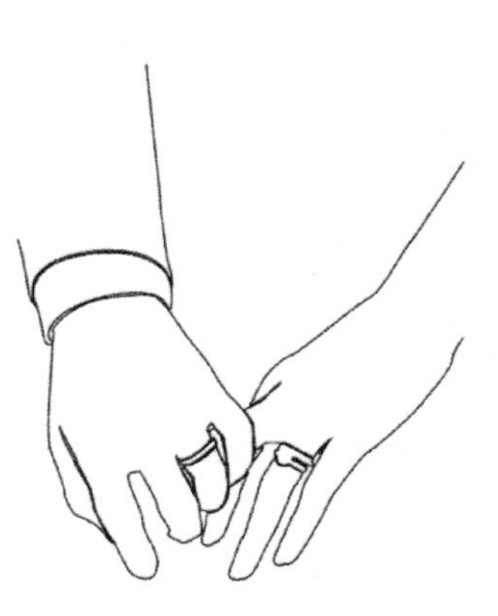

Am I naive to still see the good in you,
In your actions,
In everything ?

Probably...

I never believed in soul bonds.

At least not until you ...

I hoped to forget about you when she was here,
How could I ?

When she looks just like you.

Even if our time never comes,
I'll always love you.
Not because I love you,
Because you've given me the best gift I've ever received.
For that I'll always love you.

Maybe in another lifetime things would be different.

I try to erase the memory of you,
The flashbacks pound my chest.
Every time I close my eyes you're there,
You're in the lyrics of the songs we shared,
I walk past someone who smells the same as you and then suddenly you're everywhere I look.
I try to erase the memory of you,
There you are in her.

I'd like to think that in a different life we succeed

...

Or maybe this is how it was always supposed to be

I think it's sad,
Or maybe it's selfish ...
The only reason there is still air in my lungs,
Is for HER.
I knew without me she'd have nobody,
After all she doesn't know you.
She looks to me for guidance,
Support and comfort.
Maybe it's selfish,
I found a reason to keep breathing,
I was her whole world.
Such a bitter sweet feeling.
Maybe it's selfish but without her there would be no me.

I was never yours,
You were never mine,
So I guess in many ways this was never
supposed to work out between us ...

How did chasing my own dad for many years
turn into me chasing you to be her dad?
I told myself I wanted better for my children,
They'd grow up with two parents who loved
them dearly.
I told myself I'd have a baby with the right
person who would stick by me.
I told myself that I'd do so much differently,
Yet I've ended up doing the same thing ...

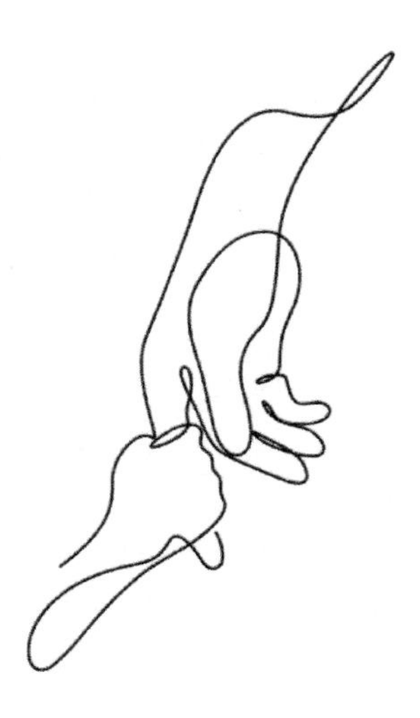

I hope you know I've never stopped caring or
loving you,
I just have nothing to say to you anymore.
I can not express my feelings anymore because
they were never valid.
I wish nothing but the best for you,
If that wasn't me or her I hope you find it.
I'll be happy for you,
From a distance.
I want you to know I've never stopped caring or
loving you.

Sometimes I look up at the beautiful setting of the sun,
Wind blowing through my hair,
Music we used to listen to playing from a far.
I look to the sky not because you're there,
Simply because it holds all of our memories.

The best thing that happened to me was
meeting you,
You took away the pain I felt for so long,
You made me believe in love again,
You gave me HER.
The best thing that happened to me was
meeting you,
You broke my heart so that no man would
ever be able to again,
You made me hate the idea of love,
But you gave me her the only love I ever need.

Moving on from you while still loving you and
wanting things to work.
Well that was one of the hardest things I have
ever had to do.
You definitely didn't make that easy, neither
of us did.

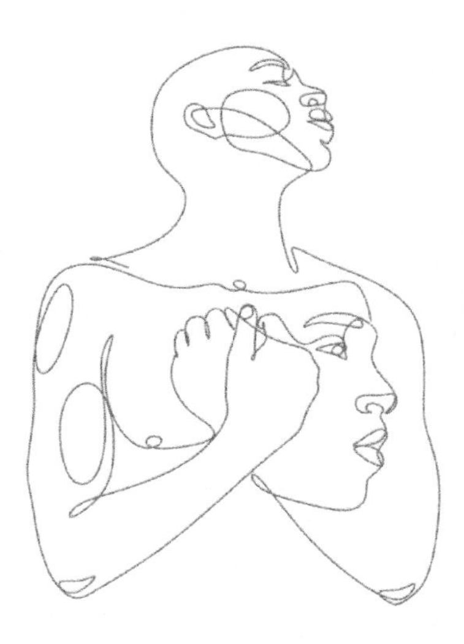

I'll be sure to tell her when she asks.
When she asks me those dreaded questions of
where you are,
I'll be sure to tell her.
I won't break her heart with the harshness,
I'll tell her my truth.
When she asks me those gut wrenching questions
of where you are,
I'll be sure to tell her.
I'll simply tell her the truth.
You wasn't ready to have a baby,
The thought of failure petrified you,
The option to grow up isn't something you was
ready for when I told you I was pregnant.
I'll never let her know the harshness you told me.
I know it was said out of anger and frustration,
I'll never let her know she isn't loved by anyone.

Please don't keep pushing me away and
expecting to find me in the same place you
left me.
Once it's done for good you'll never find that
version of me again.
No matter how hard you search.

Im allowed to give myself time to grieve.
Grieve what could've been.

I write about our love,
or rather my love for you
So that it'll never die.

When you say move on,
Is that what you really want ?

I ask because you keep coming back.

My breathing becomes lighter when you're not around.

Each time you come back,
It hurts less when you leave.

The words that leave your lips must be lies,
Your actions don't match your words.
You can't say you miss me
While acting like you hate me.

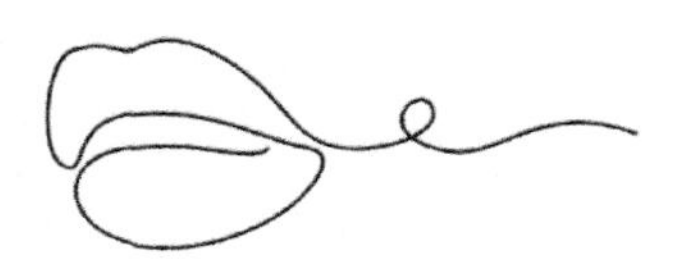

It was never about needing you,
It was always about wanting you.
And I can't even begging to explain why.

I hurt you,
You hurt me,
We can't change what's happened.
It is what it is

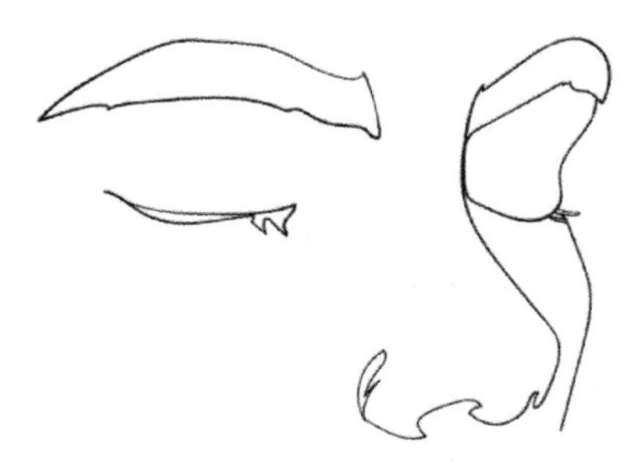

I think deep down it's not a case of you
wanting to find better than us,
I think it's a case of you not knowing how to be
better for us.

I don't think I'll ever truly get over you,
Get over what happened.

I think we were just two damaged children
craving love and validation,
In doing so we created another life.
It tested me but healed my open wounds,
It tested you but cut you open more.
I think that's the thing with damaged love,
Sometimes you just don't know how to love.

I still think about you
With every sunrise
With every sunset.

Though a passing thought,
I still think about you

You may not say much,
But your eyes say everything.

I guess that's why I find things hard to believe

I think slowly I began to get over you,
Not because I don't love you,
But because if we really was what you wanted you'd be here.
I think I slowly began to get over you,
Not because I wanted to,
But because my life is moving forward with our child.

I pray one day it's not too late
for you to see everything you've missed out on.

Months I spent trying to figure you out
Questioning why
But honestly I'm tired.
I can't change what's happened,
We can only change what happens.

I've questioned many things recently
One being why it was you to be her dad.
I made peace with all the losses of little fingers
and toes I'd experienced,
Something I didn't tell many people.

So why you ?
Why was you destined to be her dad.

I've wondered many many times why you.
It's not like we were trying or even ready
So why you ?

I don't know why.

I think maybe it was always supposed to be you,
You were always supposed to give her to me.

The more I say I love you,
The more it sounds like I'm trying to
convince myself that maybe that's true.

For her sake please let me break the toxic cycle,
Let me go,
Let me move on,
Let me break the toxic cycle before she thinks it's normal.
If our time isn't yet,
Leave me alone until our time comes.
If it ever does.

See me and you we're different
I hate when people talk bad about you,
I don't talk bad about you.
You allow people to talk bad about me.
You too also talk bad about me
This is why me and you are different.
I defend you,
You shame me.

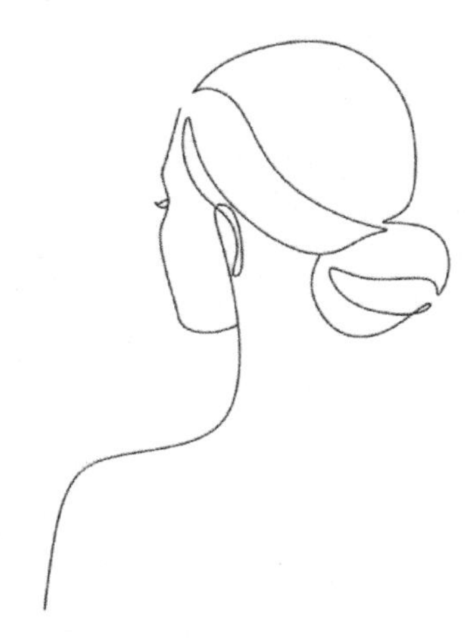

It made me sick to my stomach
To see you talk to other women about me
Call me crazy,
Allow people to talk bad about me
About OUR child.
It made me sick to my stomach
All while you didn't even bat an eyelid
That's what hurt the most.

Afterword

The past 2 years I've faced many trials and tribulations, regarding a very vulnerable time in a woman's life. through writing I have found a way to express my emotions and really let go and cope with a of a lot of pain.

This particular poetry book is about my time as a first time mum and the pregnancy, it also really touches base on having a baby with the wrong person. This is something a lot of women will be able to relate to and interpret to their own lives. Through my time of writing and engaging with other women who shared some of their stories with me I was able to capture a raw sense of emotion and put that in to a modern take on poetry.

Find out more – www.Anisian Publishing.com

Printed in Great Britain
by Amazon

27412709R00056